SCHOLASTIC

D0841850

EASY SIMULATIONS

HOW A BILL BECOMES A LAW

by Pat Luce
& Holly Joyner

New York • Toronto • London • Auckland • Sydney
Mexico City • New Delhi • Hong Kong • Buenos Aires

Teaching *Resources*

Scholastic Inc. grants teachers permission to photocopy the activity sheets from this book for classroom use.
No other part of this publication may be reproduced in whole or in part, or stored in a retrieval system, or transmitted in
any form or by any means, electronic, mechanical, photocopying, recording, or otherwise, without written permission of the publisher.
For information regarding permission, write to Scholastic Inc., 557 Broadway, New York, NY 10012.

Editors: Tim Bailey, Maria L. Chang
Cover design by Jason Robinson
Cover illustration by Doug Knutson
Interior design by Holly Grundon

ISBN-13: 978-0-439-62573-9
ISBN-10: 0-439-62573-4
Copyright © 2008 by Pat Luce and Holly Joyner
All rights reserved.
Printed in the U.S.A.

3 4 5 6 7 8 9 10   40   15 14 13 12

Contents

"Impress upon children the truth that the exercise of the elective franchise is a social duty of as solemn a nature as man can be called to perform; that a man may not innocently trifle with his vote; that every elector is a trustee as well for others as himself and that every measure he supports has an important bearing on the interests of others as well as on his own."

—Daniel Webster, *The Works of Daniel Webster, Vol. II, p. 108*
(Boston: Little, Brown, and Company, 1853)

Teaching students how the foundations of our government work and how laws are made in this country is a very important—and potentially complicated—task. One powerful teaching method you can use is a class simulation. Students learn most when they see a purpose to an activity, are engaged in the learning process, and are having fun. Children love to role-play, and they do it naturally. Why not tap into their imaginations and creativity and teach them by engaging them in a simulation?

What Is a Simulation?

A simulation is a teacher-directed, student-driven activity that provides lifelike problem-solving experiences through role-playing or reenacting. Simulations use an incredible range of powerful teaching strategies. Students will acquire a rich and deep understanding of our government that is impossible to gain through the use of any textbook and develop critical-thinking skills while working collaboratively in the subject areas of civics and government and language arts. They will take responsibility for their own learning and apply skills to solve the problems that they encounter. In addition, simulations motivate *all* of your students to participate because what is required of them is fully supported by their teammates and you.

Easy Simulations: How a Bill Becomes a Law is designed to teach students about how our government works by inviting them to become participants in the legislative system. Over the course of five days, they will re-create the process of considering, writing, presenting, and passing bills into law. First, students will work together as concerned citizens who see the need for new laws to be passed. After writing letters to their Senators and Representatives, students change roles to become legislators who turn those letters into proposed bills and go through the step-by-step process of turning a bill into a law. They will thoughtfully discuss and debate issues during mock congressional sessions. They will see our government's system of checks and balances in action as they deal with presidential vetoes and learn that all laws must pass constitutional muster with the Supreme Court. After the simulation is over, they will write a final "Congressional Record" entry and describe their experiences during the simulation. You can use this entry as an assessment tool to determine what students have learned and the success of the simulation.

Conducting the Simulation

This book provides an easy-to-use guide for running a five-day simulation—everything you need to create an educational experience that your students will talk about for a very long time. You will find background information for both you and your students that describes the history and workings of the United States government, and in particular, the legislative process. You'll also find some primary documents, such as the United States Constitution, the Bill of Rights, and an actual House bill, plus examples of bills written by real students. You may want to photocopy and distribute these pages to students before starting the simulation.

This simulation is divided into five "episodes"—one for each day of the school week—each one taking students through the process of how a bill becomes a law. Consider starting the simulation on a Monday so that it will run its course by Friday. Complete all preparatory work (i.e., building background knowledge) during the prior week. Each episode should take about 45 to 90 minutes, depending on your class size.

Before you begin the simulation, be certain to read through the entire book so you can familiarize yourself with how a simulation works and prepare any materials that you may need. Feel free to supplement with photos, illustrations, videos, music, and any other details that will enhance the experience for you and your students. Enjoy!

SETTING THE SCENE:
The Law of the Land

The United States Constitution is the "Supreme Law of the Land." Every citizen is protected by, and required to abide by, what is written in this document. Even though the Constitution is more than 200 years old, it is a "living document"—it can be amended and interpreted to deal with issues and problems that our forefathers, who wrote the original, could never have anticipated.

At its core, the Constitution is a framework for our country's government and provides for the rights and protection of its citizens. But how did these ideas begin? Let's look back about 2,500 years, when the ancient Greeks developed a system in which every male citizen voted on what was best for their people. One of their greatest leaders, Pericles, wrote about this form of government saying, "It is called democracy, for the administration is in the hands of the many and not of the few." (The word *democracy* means "rule of the people.") Now fast-forward 1,700 years to medieval England. In 1215, King John was forced by a group of English barons to approve a set of laws that would guarantee the rights of Englishmen and that the king himself would have to obey. This set of laws, called the Magna Carta, introduced the idea that people had rights and that even the king was not above the rule of law. British philosopher John Locke went even further and argued that people are the source of power, not kings.

Four hundred years after the Magna Carta was written, a small group of English settlers arrived in America and started a new colony in Plymouth, Massachusetts. These colonists, known today as the Pilgrims, wrote a set of rules to govern their new colony. The Mayflower Compact, written in 1620 by the Pilgrims onboard the *Mayflower*, stated that all adult males who are settling in Plymouth had the right to vote on issues. The men would assemble in town meetings and make their own laws. This was the first example of majority-ruled democratic government in America.

How a Bill Becomes a Law © 2008 by Pat Luce and Holly Joyner, Scholastic Teaching Resources

American settlers, however, were still under England's rule. When the British parliament started passing laws and taxing the Americans without representation from the colonies, the Americans began to rebel. In 1776, Thomas Jefferson expressed the feeling of many of his countrymen in the Declaration of Independence when he wrote, "All men are created equal." The ideas of equality under the law and a government meant to protect that equality were the foundations on which the American government was to be based. However, turning these ideals into practice would not be easy.

After winning the Revolutionary War, Americans wanted to make sure that they would never have to worry about one person—a king—ever telling them how to run their country. The Second Continental Congress came together to write a document designed to give individual states most of the power and the *federal* (central) government very little power. This document was called the Articles of Confederation, and it was *ratified* (approved) in 1781. Almost immediately people began to see problems with this kind of government. Many agreed that the Articles of Confederation needed to be fixed. By 1787 people were calling for an overhaul of the Articles. When representatives from various states gathered in Philadelphia on May 25, 1787, everyone assumed that they would be fixing that document. Instead they created a totally new form of government.

One of the major architects of this new form of government was 36-year-old James Madison of Virginia. The representatives from Virginia, including Madison, came to the Constitutional Convention with a plan for a new kind of government comprised of three branches— executive, legislative, and judicial. All three branches would share power in a system of checks and balances, which would ensure that no one branch was more powerful than the other two. Many issues were hotly debated during the Constitutional Convention, but a draft of the Constitution was finally finished on August 6, 1787. On July 2, 1788, the Constitution of the United States of America was ratified, and James Madison secured his place in history as "the Father of the Constitution."

The Constitution, however, was not quite finished. Although the Constitution had established a government, it had not given any rights or protection to its citizens. James Monroe was determined that this oversight would be corrected. On December 15, 1791, the first ten amendments to the Constitution, known as the Bill of Rights, were passed, protecting the rights of the people of the United States.

How a Bill Becomes a Law © 2008 by Pat Luce and Holly Joyner, Scholastic Teaching Resources

The Constitution of the United States

A TRANSCRIPTION

(The following text is a transcription of the Constitution in its original form.
Italicized text have since been amended or superseded.)

We the People of the United States, in Order to form a more perfect Union, establish Justice, insure domestic Tranquility, provide for the common defence, promote the general Welfare, and secure the Blessings of Liberty to ourselves and our Posterity, do ordain and establish this Constitution for the United States of America.

ARTICLE. I.

Section. 1.

All legislative Powers herein granted shall be vested in a Congress of the United States, which shall consist of a Senate and House of Representatives.

Section. 2.

The House of Representatives shall be composed of Members chosen every second Year by the People of the several States, and the Electors in each State shall have the Qualifications requisite for Electors of the most numerous Branch of the State Legislature.

No Person shall be a Representative who shall not have attained to the Age of twenty five Years, and been seven Years a Citizen of the United States, and who shall not, when elected, be an Inhabitant of that State in which he shall be chosen.

Representatives and direct Taxes shall be apportioned among the several States which may be included within this Union, according to their respective Numbers, which shall be determined by adding to the whole Number of free Persons, including those bound to Service for a Term of Years, and excluding Indians not taxed, three fifths of all other Persons. The actual Enumeration shall be made within three Years after the first Meeting of the Congress of the United States, and within every subsequent Term of ten Years, in such Manner as they shall by Law direct. The Number of Representatives shall not exceed one for every thirty Thousand, but each State shall have at Least one Representative; and until such enumeration shall be made, the State of New Hampshire shall be entitled to chuse three, Massachusetts eight, Rhode-Island and Providence Plantations one, Connecticut five, New-York six, New Jersey four, Pennsylvania eight, Delaware one, Maryland six, Virginia ten, North Carolina five, South Carolina five, and Georgia three.

When vacancies happen in the Representation from any State, the Executive Authority thereof shall issue Writs of Election to fill such Vacancies.

The House of Representatives shall chuse their Speaker and other Officers; and shall have the sole Power of Impeachment.

Section. 3.

The Senate of the United States shall be composed of two Senators from each State, *chosen by the Legislature* thereof for six Years; and each Senator shall have one Vote.

Immediately after they shall be assembled in Consequence of the first Election, they shall be divided as equally as may be into three Classes. The Seats of the Senators of the first Class shall be vacated at the Expiration of the second Year, of the second Class at the Expiration of the fourth Year, and of the third Class at the Expiration of the sixth Year, so that one third may be chosen every second Year; *and if Vacancies happen by Resignation, or otherwise, during the Recess of the Legislature of any State, the Executive thereof may make temporary Appointments until the next Meeting of the Legislature, which shall then fill such Vacancies.*

No Person shall be a Senator who shall not have attained to the Age of thirty Years, and been nine Years a Citizen of the United States, and who shall not, when elected, be an Inhabitant of that State for which he shall be chosen.

The Vice President of the United States shall be President of the Senate, but shall have no Vote, unless they be equally divided.

The Senate shall chuse their other Officers, and also a President pro tempore, in the Absence of the Vice President, or when he shall exercise the Office of President of the United States.

The Senate shall have the sole Power to try all Impeachments. When sitting for that Purpose, they shall be on Oath or Affirmation. When the President of the United States is tried, the Chief Justice shall preside: And no Person shall be convicted without the Concurrence of two thirds of the Members present.

Judgment in Cases of Impeachment shall not extend further than to removal from Office, and disqualification to hold and enjoy any Office of honor, Trust or Profit under the United States: but the Party convicted shall nevertheless be liable and subject to Indictment, Trial, Judgment and Punishment, according to Law.

Section. 4.

The Times, Places and Manner of holding Elections for Senators and Representatives, shall be prescribed in each State by the Legislature thereof; but the Congress may at any time by Law make or alter such Regulations, except as to the Places of chusing Senators.

The Congress shall assemble at least once in every Year, and such Meeting shall *be on the first Monday in December*, unless they shall by Law appoint a different Day.

Section. 5.

Each House shall be the Judge of the Elections, Returns and Qualifications of its own Members, and a Majority of each shall constitute a Quorum to do Business; but a smaller Number may adjourn from day to day, and may be authorized to compel the Attendance of absent Members, in such Manner, and under such Penalties as each House may provide.

Each House may determine the Rules of its Proceedings, punish its Members for disorderly Behaviour, and, with the Concurrence of two thirds, expel a Member.

Each House shall keep a Journal of its Proceedings, and from time to time publish the same, excepting such Parts as may in their Judgment require Secrecy; and the Yeas and Nays of the Members of either House on any question shall, at the Desire of one fifth of those Present, be entered on the Journal.

Neither House, during the Session of Congress, shall, without the Consent of the other, adjourn for more than three days, nor to any other Place than that in which the two Houses shall be sitting.

Section. 6.

The Senators and Representatives shall receive a Compensation for their Services, to be ascertained by Law, and paid out of the Treasury of the United States. They shall in all Cases, except Treason, Felony and Breach of the Peace, be privileged from Arrest during their Attendance at the Session of their respective Houses, and in going to and returning from the same; and for any Speech or Debate in either House, they shall not be questioned in any other Place.

No Senator or Representative shall, during the Time for which he was elected, be appointed to any civil Office under the Authority of the United States, which shall have been created, or the Emoluments whereof shall have been encreased during such time; and no Person holding any Office under the United States, shall be a Member of either House during his Continuance in Office.

Section. 7.

All Bills for raising Revenue shall originate in the House of Representatives; but the Senate may propose or concur with Amendments as on other Bills.

Every Bill which shall have passed the House of Representatives and the Senate, shall, before it become a Law, be presented to the President of the United States: If he approve he shall sign it, but if not he shall return it, with his Objections to that House in which it shall have originated, who shall enter the Objections at large on their Journal, and proceed to reconsider it. If after such Reconsideration two thirds of that House shall agree to pass the Bill, it shall be sent, together with the Objections, to the other House, by which it shall likewise be reconsidered, and if approved by two thirds of that House, it shall become a Law. But in all such Cases the Votes of both Houses shall be determined by yeas and Nays, and the Names of the Persons voting for and against the Bill shall be entered on the Journal of each House respectively. If any Bill shall not be returned by the President within ten Days (Sundays excepted) after it shall have been presented to him, the Same shall be a Law, in like Manner as if he had signed it, unless the Congress by their Adjournment prevent its Return, in which Case it shall not be a Law.

Every Order, Resolution, or Vote to which the Concurrence of the Senate and House of Representatives may be necessary (except on a question of Adjournment) shall be presented to the President of the United States; and before the Same shall take Effect, shall be approved by him, or being disapproved by him, shall be repassed by two thirds of the Senate and House of Representatives, according to the Rules and Limitations prescribed in the Case of a Bill.

Section. 8.

The Congress shall have Power To lay and collect Taxes, Duties, Imposts and Excises, to pay the Debts and provide for the common Defence and general Welfare of the United States; but all Duties, Imposts and Excises shall be uniform throughout the United States;

To borrow Money on the credit of the United States;

To regulate Commerce with foreign Nations, and among the several States, and with the Indian Tribes;

To establish an uniform Rule of Naturalization, and uniform Laws on the subject of Bankruptcies throughout the United States;

To coin Money, regulate the Value thereof, and of foreign Coin, and fix the Standard of Weights and Measures;

To provide for the Punishment of counterfeiting the Securities and current Coin of the United States;

To establish Post Offices and post Roads;

To promote the Progress of Science and useful Arts, by securing for limited Times to Authors and Inventors the exclusive Right to their respective Writings and Discoveries;

To constitute Tribunals inferior to the supreme Court;

To define and punish Piracies and Felonies committed on the high Seas, and Offences against the Law of Nations;

To declare War, grant Letters of Marque and Reprisal, and make Rules concerning Captures on Land and Water;

To raise and support Armies, but no Appropriation of Money to that Use shall be for a longer Term than two Years;

To provide and maintain a Navy;

To make Rules for the Government and Regulation of the land and naval Forces;

To provide for calling forth the Militia to execute the Laws of the Union, suppress Insurrections and repel Invasions;

To provide for organizing, arming, and disciplining, the Militia, and for governing such Part of them as may be employed in the Service of the United States, reserving to the States respectively, the Appointment of the Officers, and the Authority of training the Militia according to the discipline prescribed by Congress;

To exercise exclusive Legislation in all Cases whatsoever, over such District (not exceeding ten Miles square) as may, by Cession of particular States, and the Acceptance of Congress, become the Seat of the Government of the United States, and to exercise like Authority over all Places purchased by the Consent of the Legislature of the State in which the Same shall be, for the Erection of Forts, Magazines, Arsenals, dock-Yards, and other needful Buildings;—And

To make all Laws which shall be necessary and proper for carrying into Execution the foregoing Powers, and all other Powers vested by this Constitution in the Government of the United States, or in any Department or Officer thereof.

Section. 9.

The Migration or Importation of such Persons as any of the States now existing shall think proper to admit, shall not be prohibited by the Congress prior to the Year one thousand eight hundred and eight, but a Tax or duty may be imposed on such Importation, not exceeding ten dollars for each Person.

The Privilege of the Writ of Habeas Corpus shall not be suspended, unless when in Cases of Rebellion or Invasion the public Safety may require it.

No Bill of Attainder or ex post facto Law shall be passed.

No Capitation, or other direct, Tax shall be laid, *unless in Proportion to the Census or enumeration herein before directed to be taken.*

No Tax or Duty shall be laid on Articles exported from any State.

No Preference shall be given by any Regulation of Commerce or Revenue to the Ports of one State over those of another; nor shall Vessels bound to, or from, one State, be obliged to enter, clear, or pay Duties in another.

No Money shall be drawn from the Treasury, but in Consequence of Appropriations made by Law; and a regular Statement and Account of the Receipts and Expenditures of all public Money shall be published from time to time.

No Title of Nobility shall be granted by the United States: And no Person holding any Office of Profit or Trust under them, shall, without the Consent of the Congress, accept of any present, Emolument, Office, or Title, of any kind whatever, from any King, Prince, or foreign State.

Section. 10.

No State shall enter into any Treaty, Alliance, or Confederation; grant Letters of Marque and Reprisal; coin Money; emit Bills of Credit; make any Thing but gold and silver Coin a Tender in Payment of Debts; pass any Bill of Attainder, ex post facto Law, or Law impairing the Obligation of Contracts, or grant any Title of Nobility.

No State shall, without the Consent of the Congress, lay any Imposts or Duties on Imports or Exports, except what may be absolutely necessary for executing it's inspection Laws: and the net Produce of all Duties and Imposts, laid by any State on Imports or Exports, shall be for the Use of the Treasury of the United States; and all such Laws shall be subject to the Revision and Controul of the Congress.

No State shall, without the Consent of Congress, lay any Duty of Tonnage, keep Troops, or Ships of War in time of Peace, enter into any Agreement or Compact with another State, or with a foreign Power, or engage in War, unless actually invaded, or in such imminent Danger as will not admit of delay.

ARTICLE. II.

Section. 1.

The executive Power shall be vested in a President of the United States of America. He shall hold his Office during the Term of four Years, and, together with the Vice President, chosen for the same Term, be elected, as follows:

Each State shall appoint, in such Manner as the Legislature thereof may direct, a Number of Electors, equal to the whole Number of Senators and Representatives to which the State may be entitled in the Congress: but no Senator or Representative, or Person holding an Office of Trust or Profit under the United States, shall be appointed an Elector.

The Electors shall meet in their respective States, and vote by Ballot for two Persons, of whom one at least shall not be an Inhabitant of the same State with themselves. And they shall make a List of all the Persons voted for, and of the Number of Votes for each; which List they shall sign and certify, and transmit sealed to the Seat of the Government of the United States, directed to the President of the Senate. The President of the Senate shall, in the Presence of the Senate and House of Representatives, open all the Certificates, and the Votes shall then be counted. The Person having the greatest Number of Votes shall be the President, if such Number be a Majority of the whole Number of Electors appointed; and if there be more than one who have such Majority, and have an equal Number of Votes, then the House of Representatives shall immediately chuse by Ballot one of them for President; and if no Person have a Majority, then from the five highest on the List the said House shall in like Manner chuse the President. But in chusing the President, the Votes shall be taken by States, the Representation from each State having one Vote; A quorum for this purpose shall consist of a Member or Members from two thirds of the States, and a Majority of all the States shall be necessary to a Choice. In every Case, after the Choice of the President, the Person having the greatest Number of Votes of the Electors shall be the Vice President. But if there should remain two or more who have equal Votes, the Senate shall chuse from them by Ballot the Vice President.

The Congress may determine the Time of chusing the Electors, and the Day on which they shall give their Votes; which Day shall be the same throughout the United States.

No Person except a natural born Citizen, or a Citizen of the United States, at the time of the Adoption of this Constitution, shall be eligible to the Office of President; neither shall any

Person be eligible to that Office who shall not have attained to the Age of thirty five Years, and been fourteen Years a Resident within the United States.

In Case of the Removal of the President from Office, or of his Death, Resignation, or Inability to discharge the Powers and Duties of the said Office, the Same shall devolve on the Vice President, and the Congress may by Law provide for the Case of Removal, Death, Resignation or Inability, both of the President and Vice President, declaring what Officer shall then act as President, and such Officer shall act accordingly, until the Disability be removed, or a President shall be elected.

The President shall, at stated Times, receive for his Services, a Compensation, which shall neither be increased nor diminished during the Period for which he shall have been elected, and he shall not receive within that Period any other Emolument from the United States, or any of them.

Before he enter on the Execution of his Office, he shall take the following Oath or Affirmation:— "I do solemnly swear (or affirm) that I will faithfully execute the Office of President of the United States, and will to the best of my Ability, preserve, protect and defend the Constitution of the United States."

Section. 2.

The President shall be Commander in Chief of the Army and Navy of the United States, and of the Militia of the several States, when called into the actual Service of the United States; he may require the Opinion, in writing, of the principal Officer in each of the executive Departments, upon any Subject relating to the Duties of their respective Offices, and he shall have Power to grant Reprieves and Pardons for Offences against the United States, except in Cases of Impeachment.

He shall have Power, by and with the Advice and Consent of the Senate, to make Treaties, provided two thirds of the Senators present concur; and he shall nominate, and by and with the Advice and Consent of the Senate, shall appoint Ambassadors, other public Ministers and Consuls, Judges of the supreme Court, and all other Officers of the United States, whose Appointments are not herein otherwise provided for, and which shall be established by Law: but the Congress may by Law vest the Appointment of such inferior Officers, as they think proper, in the President alone, in the Courts of Law, or in the Heads of Departments.

The President shall have Power to fill up all Vacancies that may happen during the Recess of the Senate, by granting Commissions which shall expire at the End of their next Session.

Section. 3.

He shall from time to time give to the Congress Information of the State of the Union, and recommend to their Consideration such Measures as he shall judge necessary and expedient; he may, on extraordinary Occasions, convene both Houses, or either of them, and in Case of Disagreement between them, with Respect to the Time of Adjournment, he may adjourn them to such Time as he shall think proper; he shall receive Ambassadors and other public Ministers; he shall take Care that the Laws be faithfully executed, and shall Commission all the Officers of the United States.

Section. 4.

The President, Vice President and all civil Officers of the United States, shall be removed from Office on Impeachment for, and Conviction of, Treason, Bribery, or other high Crimes and Misdemeanors.

ARTICLE III.

Section. 1.

The judicial Power of the United States shall be vested in one supreme Court, and in such inferior Courts as the Congress may from time to time ordain and establish. The Judges, both of the supreme and inferior Courts, shall hold their Offices during good Behaviour, and shall, at stated Times, receive for their Services a Compensation, which shall not be diminished during their Continuance in Office.

Section. 2.

The judicial Power shall extend to all Cases, in Law and Equity, arising under this Constitution, the Laws of the United States, and Treaties made, or which shall be made, under their Authority;—to all Cases affecting Ambassadors, other public Ministers and Consuls;—to all Cases of admiralty and maritime Jurisdiction;—to Controversies to which the United States shall be a Party;—to Controversies between two or more States;— *between a State and Citizens of another State*;—between Citizens of different States;—between Citizens of the same State claiming Lands under Grants of different States, and between a State, or the Citizens thereof, and foreign States, Citizens or Subjects.

In all Cases affecting Ambassadors, other public Ministers and Consuls, and those in which a State shall be Party, the supreme Court shall have original Jurisdiction. In all the other Cases before mentioned, the supreme Court shall have appellate Jurisdiction, both as to Law and Fact, with such Exceptions, and under such Regulations as the Congress shall make.

The Trial of all Crimes, except in Cases of Impeachment, shall be by Jury; and such Trial shall be held in the State where the said Crimes shall have been committed; but when not committed within any State, the Trial shall be at such Place or Places as the Congress may by Law have directed.

Section. 3.

Treason against the United States, shall consist only in levying War against them, or in adhering to their Enemies, giving them Aid and Comfort. No Person shall be convicted of Treason unless on the Testimony of two Witnesses to the same overt Act, or on Confession in open Court.

The Congress shall have Power to declare the Punishment of Treason, but no Attainder of Treason shall work Corruption of Blood, or Forfeiture except during the Life of the Person attainted.

ARTICLE. IV.

Section. 1.

Full Faith and Credit shall be given in each State to the public Acts, Records, and judicial Proceedings of every other State. And the Congress may by general Laws prescribe the Manner in which such Acts, Records and Proceedings shall be proved, and the Effect thereof.

Section. 2.

The Citizens of each State shall be entitled to all Privileges and Immunities of Citizens in the several States.

A Person charged in any State with Treason, Felony, or other Crime, who shall flee from Justice, and be found in another State, shall on Demand of the executive Authority of the State from which he fled, be delivered up, to be removed to the State having Jurisdiction of the Crime.

No Person held to Service or Labour in one State, under the Laws thereof, escaping into another, shall, in Consequence of any Law or Regulation therein, be discharged from such Service or Labour, but shall be delivered up on Claim of the Party to whom such Service or Labour may be due.

Section. 3.

New States may be admitted by the Congress into this Union; but no new State shall be formed or erected within the Jurisdiction of any other State; nor any State be formed by the Junction of two or more States, or Parts of States, without the Consent of the Legislatures of the States concerned as well as of the Congress.

The Congress shall have Power to dispose of and make all needful Rules and Regulations respecting the Territory or other Property belonging to the United States; and nothing in this Constitution shall be so construed as to Prejudice any Claims of the United States, or of any particular State.

Section. 4.

The United States shall guarantee to every State in this Union a Republican Form of Government, and shall protect each of them against Invasion; and on Application of the Legislature, or of the Executive (when the Legislature cannot be convened), against domestic Violence.

ARTICLE. V.

The Congress, whenever two thirds of both Houses shall deem it necessary, shall propose Amendments to this Constitution, or, on the Application of the Legislatures of two thirds of the several States, shall call a Convention for proposing Amendments, which, in either Case, shall be valid to all Intents and Purposes, as Part of this Constitution, when ratified by the Legislatures of three fourths of the several States, or by Conventions in three fourths thereof, as the one or the other Mode of Ratification may be proposed by the Congress; Provided that no Amendment which may be made prior to the Year One thousand eight hundred and eight shall in any Manner affect the first and fourth Clauses in the Ninth Section of the first Article; and that no State, without its Consent, shall be deprived of its equal Suffrage in the Senate.

ARTICLE. VI.

All Debts contracted and Engagements entered into, before the Adoption of this Constitution, shall be as valid against the United States under this Constitution, as under the Confederation.

This Constitution, and the Laws of the United States which shall be made in Pursuance thereof; and all Treaties made, or which shall be made, under the Authority of the United States, shall be the supreme Law of the Land; and the Judges in every State shall be bound thereby, any Thing in the Constitution or Laws of any State to the Contrary notwithstanding.

The Senators and Representatives before mentioned, and the Members of the several State Legislatures, and all executive and judicial Officers, both of the United States and of the several States, shall be bound by Oath or Affirmation, to support this Constitution; but no religious Test shall ever be required as a Qualification to any Office or public Trust under the United States.

ARTICLE. VII.

The Ratification of the Conventions of nine States, shall be sufficient for the Establishment of this Constitution between the States so ratifying the Same.

The Word, "the," being interlined between the seventh and eighth Lines of the first Page, the Word "Thirty" being partly written on an Erazure in the fifteenth Line of the first Page, The Words "is tried" being interlined between the thirty second and thirty third Lines of the first Page and the Word "the" being interlined between the forty third and forty fourth Lines of the second Page.

Attest William Jackson Secretary

Done in Convention by the Unanimous Consent of the States present the Seventeenth Day of September in the Year of our Lord one thousand seven hundred and Eighty seven and of the Independence of the United States of America the Twelfth In witness whereof We have hereunto subscribed our Names,

G. Washington
Presidt and deputy from Virginia

DELAWARE
Geo: Read
Gunning Bedford jun
John Dickinson
Richard Bassett
Jaco: Broom

MARYLAND
James McHenry
Dan of St Thos. Jenifer
Danl. Carroll

VIRGINIA
John Blair
James Madison Jr.

NORTH CAROLINA
Wm. Blount
Richd. Dobbs Spaight
Hu Williamson

SOUTH CAROLINA
J. Rutledge
Charles Cotesworth Pinckney
Charles Pinckney
Pierce Butler

GEORGIA
William Few
Abr Baldwin

NEW HAMPSHIRE
John Langdon
Nicholas Gilman

MASSACHUSETTS
Nathaniel Gorham
Rufus King

CONNECTICUT
Wm. Saml. Johnson
Roger Sherman

NEW YORK
Alexander Hamilton

NEW JERSEY
Wil: Livingston
David Brearley
Wm. Paterson
Jona: Dayton

PENNSYLVANIA
B Franklin
Thomas Mifflin
Robt. Morris
Geo. Clymer
Thos. FitzSimons
Jared Ingersoll
James Wilson
Gouv Morris

Source: http://www.archives.gov/national-archives-experience/charters/constitution.html

The Bill of Rights

A Transcription

(The following text is a transcription of the first ten amendments
to the Constitution in their original form.)

THE PREAMBLE TO THE BILL OF RIGHTS

Congress of the United States
begun and held at the City of New York, on
Wednesday the fourth of March, one thousand seven hundred and eighty nine.

THE Conventions of a number of the States, having at the time of their adopting the
Constitution, expressed a desire, in order to prevent misconstruction or abuse of its powers,
that further declaratory and restrictive clauses should be added: And as extending the ground of
public confidence in the Government, will best ensure the beneficent ends of its institution.

RESOLVED by the Senate and House of Representatives of the United States of America,
in Congress assembled, two thirds of both Houses concurring, that the following Articles
be proposed to the Legislatures of the several States, as amendments to the Constitution of
the United States, all, or any of which Articles, when ratified by three fourths of the said
Legislatures, to be valid to all intents and purposes, as part of the said Constitution; viz.

ARTICLES in addition to, and Amendment of the Constitution of the United States of America,
proposed by Congress, and ratified by the Legislatures of the several States, pursuant to the fifth
Article of the original Constitution.

Amendment I

Congress shall make no law respecting an establishment of religion, or prohibiting the free
exercise thereof; or abridging the freedom of speech, or of the press; or the right of the people
peaceably to assemble, and to petition the Government for a redress of grievances.

Amendment II

A well regulated Militia, being necessary to the security of a free State, the right of the people to
keep and bear Arms, shall not be infringed.

Amendment III

No Soldier shall, in time of peace be quartered in any house, without the consent of the Owner,
nor in time of war, but in a manner to be prescribed by law.

Amendment IV

The right of the people to be secure in their persons, houses, papers, and effects, against unreasonable searches and seizures, shall not be violated, and no Warrants shall issue, but upon probable cause, supported by Oath or affirmation, and particularly describing the place to be searched, and the persons or things to be seized.

Amendment V

No person shall be held to answer for a capital, or otherwise infamous crime, unless on a presentment or indictment of a Grand Jury, except in cases arising in the land or naval forces, or in the Militia, when in actual service in time of War or public danger; nor shall any person be subject for the same offence to be twice put in jeopardy of life or limb; nor shall be compelled in any criminal case to be a witness against himself, nor be deprived of life, liberty, or property, without due process of law; nor shall private property be taken for public use, without just compensation.

Amendment VI

In all criminal prosecutions, the accused shall enjoy the right to a speedy and public trial, by an impartial jury of the State and district wherein the crime shall have been committed, which district shall have been previously ascertained by law, and to be informed of the nature and cause of the accusation; to be confronted with the witnesses against him; to have compulsory process for obtaining witnesses in his favor, and to have the Assistance of Counsel for his defence.

Amendment VII

In Suits at common law, where the value in controversy shall exceed twenty dollars, the right of trial by jury shall be preserved, and no fact tried by a jury, shall be otherwise re-examined in any Court of the United States, than according to the rules of the common law.

Amendment VIII

Excessive bail shall not be required, nor excessive fines imposed, nor cruel and unusual punishments inflicted.

Amendment IX

The enumeration in the Constitution, of certain rights, shall not be construed to deny or disparage others retained by the people.

Amendment X

The powers not delegated to the United States by the Constitution, nor prohibited by it to the States, are reserved to the States respectively, or to the people.

Source: http://www.archives.gov/national-archives-experience/charters/bill_of_rights.html

How a Bill Becomes a Law

The United States federal government consists of three branches—legislative, executive, and judicial. The legislative branch (Congress) makes the laws, the executive branch (the President and his or her Cabinet) carries out the laws, and the judicial branch (the Supreme Court) settles questions about the laws and makes sure that they comply with the U.S. Constitution.

Each year many proposals for new laws are introduced in both chambers of Congress—the House of Representatives and the Senate. The President and his or her administration are responsible for a large number of proposals acted on by Congress. The most common proposal is in the form of a bill. The idea for a bill may also come from an interest group, a business or corporation, a congressional committee, or a private citizen.

A bill is written with specific language and in a specific form. Once written, a Representative or Senator introduces the bill in his or her chamber. Both the House and the Senate consist of several committees that deal with specific issues. The bill is sent to the appropriate committee for consideration. The committee holds meetings where people can express what they think about the bill. After being heard and revised in committee ("marked up"), the bill is debated and voted upon in the chamber where it was introduced. If the bill is rejected, it may be amended and voted on again. If it is passed, it goes to the other chamber for consideration.

In the other chamber, the bill goes through the same committee process as in the chamber where it was introduced. If the bill passes in both the House and the Senate, it goes to the President for his or her signature. The President may sign the bill into law, or he or she may veto the bill, giving the reasons why and perhaps making recommendations for changes. At this point, Congress may override the veto if two-thirds of all Congresspersons vote for the bill. The bill is then enacted into law.

Even after a bill becomes a law, however, the Supreme Court can overturn it if the Court finds that the law contradicts the principles of the U.S. Constitution.

How a Bill Becomes a Law © 2008 by Pat Luce and Holly Joyner, Scholastic Teaching Resources

How a Bill Becomes a Law

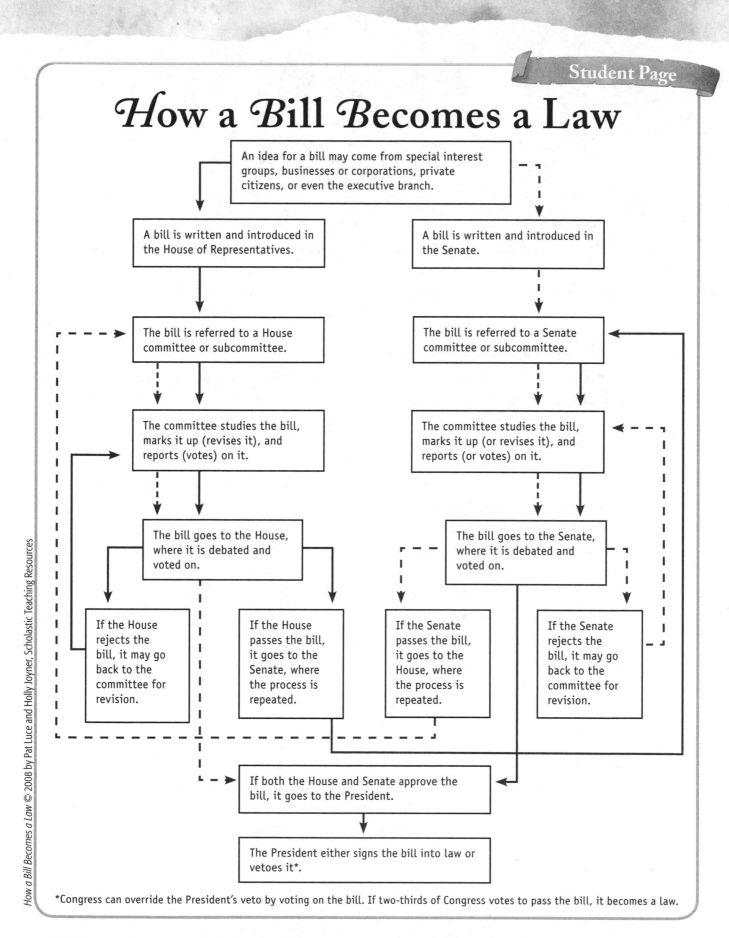

An idea for a bill may come from special interest groups, businesses or corporations, private citizens, or even the executive branch.

A bill is written and introduced in the House of Representatives.

A bill is written and introduced in the Senate.

The bill is referred to a House committee or subcommittee.

The bill is referred to a Senate committee or subcommittee.

The committee studies the bill, marks it up (revises it), and reports (votes) on it.

The committee studies the bill, marks it up (or revises it), and reports (or votes) on it.

The bill goes to the House, where it is debated and voted on.

The bill goes to the Senate, where it is debated and voted on.

If the House rejects the bill, it may go back to the committee for revision.

If the House passes the bill, it goes to the Senate, where the process is repeated.

If the Senate passes the bill, it goes to the House, where the process is repeated.

If the Senate rejects the bill, it may go back to the committee for revision.

If both the House and Senate approve the bill, it goes to the President.

The President either signs the bill into law or vetoes it*.

*Congress can override the President's veto by voting on the bill. If two-thirds of Congress votes to pass the bill, it becomes a law.

How a Bill Becomes a Law © 2008 by Pat Luce and Holly Joyner, Scholastic Teaching Resources

People Power

OVERVIEW

Students take on the roles of concerned citizens and brainstorm issues and concerns (related to school or to society as a whole) that need to be addressed. They then write a letter to their Congressperson, asking him or her to propose a bill that would address these issues.

RUNNING THE SIMULATION

One of the most important aspects of our constitutional government is that the power of the government resides in its citizens. This power can be exercised by groups with a common interest, seeking laws that will correct an injustice or provide for a need that will benefit the people as a whole.

To give students a sense of this "power of the people," invite them to brainstorm ideas for improving society or correcting issues. Use your discretion to determine the scope of this brainstorming session. For example, a class may wish to address national or even global issues, such as the environment, gun control, or immigration, or focus on local issues that affect their community. Or you might prefer to encourage students to think about areas or issues in the school that they would like to change—for example, playground safety, lunch menus, or extended recess. This option would bring the idea of creating change to a more immediate, personal level for students.

Remind students how brainstorming sessions work:

- All ideas are accepted.

- Ideas are generated instead of evaluated.

- Everyone listens to one another's ideas.

Give students about ten minutes to think independently, then invite them to share their ideas with the class. Record students' ideas on a large piece of chart paper or on the board. Be sure to allow plenty of time so everyone can add their ideas to the list.

After you have recorded everyone's ideas, ask students to look at the list and think about how you might group similar ideas together. Engage students in an open discussion to come up with overarching issues. For example, the following ideas relate to the issue of recess:

- Recess time should be longer.

- Limit the number of classes that are having recess at the same time.

- More games and equipment should be available for recess.

- Designate specific areas where various sports are played during recess.

The goal is to have enough issues so that four students could work on each one. For example, a class of 20 students would have five issues, while a class of 30 would have about seven issues.

When you have enough issues, invite students to choose the ones that interest them the most. Have each student list three issues that they would like to work on and rank them from 1 to 3, using 1 to indicate the issue he or she is most interested in. Use these rankings to assign students to various "concerned citizen groups." Each group will be responsible for a particular issue and will write a letter to their representative in Congress, requesting that a law be passed to address this issue. Tell students that their letter should clearly explain the main issue and list the ideas related to it. (Use the blank form on page 26.) Remind students that they have to write this letter as a cooperative group, seeking out the opinions of all the members of the group. Have students type or write their letters neatly, ready for presentation in the next episode. Collect the letters at the end of this episode.

TAKING IT FURTHER

It's entirely possible for a class to take any of these issues beyond the four walls of their classroom. This is how political action starts—with an idea. School issues can be taken to the student government or the principal, while community issues can be taken to civic leaders, like the mayor. Even federal and state issues can result in students writing letters that bring their concerns to officials' desks.

ACTIVITY

Have students conduct research to find out the names of your state's Representatives and Senators. To find out who your House Representative is, go to http://www.house.gov. To learn about your state's Senators, go to http://www.senate.gov.

Name: _____ Date: _____

Date _____

Dear Congressperson:

_____

_____

_____

_____

_____

_____

_____

_____

_____

_____

_____

_____

How a Bill Becomes a Law © 2008 by Pat Luce and Holly Joyner, Scholastic Teaching Resources

Seating the Congress

OVERVIEW

Students assume the roles of Senators and House Representatives from different states. They then take the letters that were written in the last episode and break up into committees that will turn those letters into proposed bills.

BEFORE YOU START

If possible, take the issues the class generated from the previous episode and create "issue cards" — lists of the students' ideas consolidated under a particular issue (see right). Type or handwrite these cards and distribute them to each committee during the episode. Students will find these cards helpful in getting them started with their thinking and writing of their bills.

Issue Card - Recess Committee

1. Is it long enough? Right length?
2. Are the rules appropriate?
3. How many classes should be outside at one time?
4. How many recesses each day?
5. What sports are allowed?
6. Is anything missing (supplies, equipment, water fountain)?
7. What are the physical boundaries?

Make photocopies of the House bill on pages 31–32. If you want to give students more examples of bills from the House and the Senate, you can download them from the Library of Congress at http://thomas.loc.gov.

BACKGROUND: THE LEGISLATIVE BRANCH

The legislative branch of our government, called Congress, creates the laws that protect and provide for the citizens. Congress is divided into two chambers—the Senate and the House of Representatives. Each member of Congress is elected by the people of his or her state.

The Senate and the House of Representatives were established during debates at the Constitutional Convention in 1787. The smaller states demanded equal representation in Congress for every state, while the larger states wanted representation to be based on a state's population. In what became known as the Great Compromise, the two chambers were created so that the Senate has equal representation, while the House of Representatives has representation by population.

The Senate consists of 100 members, with two Senators from each state. Senators are elected for six-year terms for an unlimited number of terms. Elections are staggered so that two Senators are not elected at the same time from the same state. In order to be elected as a Senator, a person must be at least 30 years old and have been a citizen of the United States for a minimum of nine years. The person must also be a resident of the state in which he or she is being elected.

The House of Representatives has 435 members. The number of representatives from each state is determined by the state's population. Every state must have at least one representative. Alaska, Delaware, North Dakota, South Dakota, Vermont, and Wyoming each have only one representative. California, on the other hand, has the most representatives—53 in all. The number of representatives from a state can change if its population changes. The Constitution requires that a census, or counting, of the country's population be taken every ten years. Members of the House of Representatives serve for two years and can be reelected any number of times. In order to be elected as a Representative, a person must be at least 25 years old and have been a citizen of the United States for at least seven years. In addition, that person must be a resident of the state for which he or she is chosen.

RUNNING THE SIMULATION

Divide the class evenly into two groups and assign one group to be the House of Representatives and the other group to be the Senate. (Another option would be to partner up with another class—one class could be the House and the other the Senate.) Allow students to choose which state they would like to represent, or if you prefer, assign each student a state. For example, a student might be a Representative from Massachusetts or a Senator from Wyoming.

When students have been assigned to a chamber and chosen a state, it's time to start the actual work of writing a bill. First, review the letters written by the various concerned citizen groups (from the last episode). You might want to read each letter aloud to remind students of the various issues that had been brought up.

Next, decide what committees need to be created to address these issues. Depending on your class size, some of the letters and issues raised in Episode 1 may not make it to committee during this session of Congress. (This situation often arises in real life. Be sure to choose those issues that seem to have the most potential for creating good conversations and debate.)

Explain to students that both the Senate and the House have several committees that specialize in particular issues. Most committees in one chamber have counterparts in the other chamber. (See page 29 for a partial list of committees in both the Senate and the House.) For example, if a bill related to reducing air pollution starts out in the House of Representatives, it will be assigned to the Committee on Natural Resources since that group is responsible for issues concerning the environment and pollution. When the bill goes to the Senate, it will be assigned to the Environment and Public Works Committee since it falls under their area of concern.

When forming committees in your class, you can use the committees on the list or create your own in the event that none of them fit your specific issues. Assign students to Congressional

Committees of the Senate
Finance Committee *(spending)*
Armed Services Committee *(national security)*
Health, Education, Labor, and Pensions Committee *(public health, education, jobs and wages)*
Commerce, Science, and Transportation Committee *(business, science, highways and public safety)*
Agriculture, Nutrition, and Forestry Committee *(food, farms, and land use)*
Foreign Relations Committee *(issues involving other countries)*
Energy and Natural Resources Committee *(energy sources, climate change, and gas and oil issues)*
Environment and Public Works Committee *(environment, pollution, highways, dams, bridges)*
Banking, Housing, and Urban Affairs Committee *(problems in cities, housing issues, and money)*

Committees of the House of Representatives
Committee on Appropriations *(spending)*
Committee on Armed Services *(national security)*
Committee on Education and Labor *(education, jobs, and wages)*
Committee on Energy and Commerce *(energy sources and business)*
Committee on Agriculture *(food, farms, and land use)*
Committee on Foreign Affairs *(issues involving other countries)*
Committee on Natural Resources *(environment and pollution)*
Committee on Transportation and Infrastructure *(highways, dams, bridges, etc.)*
Committee on Science and Technology *(science and technology issues including oversight of NASA)*

committees based on the issues they were working on in Episode 1. For example, students in the concerned citizen group who wrote about the issue of recess will now comprise the Senate's Recess Committee and will propose a bill based on this issue. Keep in mind that half of these committees will be in the Senate and the other half in the House of Representatives.

Distribute copies of the House bill (pages 31–32) to students and lead a discussion about how it's written. Ask students what they notice about the vocabulary, structure, and format of the bill. Inform students that each bill is identified by a number preceded by either H.R. for House bills or S. for Senate bills. The bill starts with a brief statement explaining its purpose ("To require an independent evaluation of distance education programs"), followed by the names of the representatives proposing the bill and the name of the committee that it was assigned to. Guide students to notice the words "Be it enacted by the Senate and House of Representatives of the United States of America in Congress assembled," which comes before the main body of the bill. Explain that this formal phrasing simply says that the bill is a legislative act and has the authority to become law.

After this discussion, distribute the letters and/or issue cards to the relevant committees. Instruct students in each committee to discuss the various ideas listed in their letter and figure out how the changes can be implemented. You might want to suggest that students divide up the tasks in their group, with each committee member assuming a different role. For example, one student could write down ideas, while another could facilitate the discussion, and the other could keep track of time, and so on. Each committee should also have a chairperson, who will read the proposed bill in the next episode.

Circulate among the different committees to listen to their ideas and, if necessary, remind students to practice respectful listening and speaking skills and to appreciate everyone's ideas. When students have reached consensus on how to present the proposed changes, they can start writing their bills. Have students use the forms on pages 33–34 (for the Senate) and pages 35–36 (for the House) to write up the official bill that will be presented to their chamber in the next episode.

ACTIVITY

Challenge students to find out more about the states that they're representing. Photocopy the letters on pages 37 (for Senators) and 38 (for House Representatives) and distribute to students. Have them conduct research and fill in the requested information about their adopted state. (You might prefer to assign this activity for homework.)

Independent Study of Distance Education Act of 2007

(Introduced in House)

110th CONGRESS

1st Session

H. R. 412

To require an independent evaluation of distance education programs.

IN THE HOUSE OF REPRESENTATIVES

January 11, 2007

Mr. EHLERS introduced the following bill; which was referred to the Committee on Education and Labor

A BILL

To require an independent evaluation of distance education programs.

Be it enacted by the Senate and House of Representatives of the United States of America in Congress assembled,

SECTION 1. SHORT TITLE.

This Act may be cited as the 'Independent Study of Distance Education Act of 2007'.

SEC. 2. INDEPENDENT EVALUATION OF DISTANCE EDUCATION PROGRAMS.

(a) Independent Evaluation – The Secretary of Education shall enter into an agreement with the National Academy of Sciences to conduct a scientifically correct, statistically valid evaluation of the quality of distance education programs, as compared to campus-based education programs, at institutions of higher education. Such evaluation shall include –

(continued on next page)

(continued)

Independent Study of Distance Education Act of 2007

(Introduced in House)

(1) identification of the elements by which the quality of distance education, as compared to campus-based education, can be assessed, including elements such as subject matter, interactivity, and student outcomes;

(2) identification of distance and campus-based education program success, with respect to student achievement, in relation to the mission of the institution of higher education; and

(3) by assessing elements including access to higher education, job placement rates, undergraduate graduation rates, and graduate and professional degree attainment rates, identification of the types of students (including classification of types of students based on student age) —

(A) who most benefit from distance education programs;

(B) who most benefit from campus-based education programs; and

(C) who do not benefit from distance education programs.

(b) Scope – The National Academy of Sciences shall select for participation in the evaluation under subsection (a) a diverse group of institutions of higher education with respect to size, mission, and geographic distribution.

(c) Interim and Final Reports – The agreement under subsection (a) shall require that the National Academy of Sciences submit to the Secretary of Education, the Committee on Health, Education, Labor and Pensions of the Senate, and the Committee on Education and Labor of the House of Representatives —

(1) an interim report regarding the evaluation under subsection (a) not later than six months after the date of enactment of this Act; and

(2) a final report regarding such evaluation not later than one year after the date of enactment of this Act.

100th Mock Congress
1st Session

S. _____
(number)

To _____

_____
(purpose of the bill)

In the Senate of the United States

_____
(date)

Presented by the _____
(committee name)

A Bill

Be it enacted by the Senate and House of Representatives of the United States of America in Congress assembled,

_____

_____

_____

_____

_____

_____

(continued on next page)

How a Bill Becomes a Law © 2008 by Pat Luce and Holly Joyner, Scholastic Teaching Resources

(continued)

100th Mock Congress
1st Session

_____

_____

_____

_____

_____

_____

_____

_____

The Senator from   The Senator from

_____   _____

The Senator from   The Senator from

_____   _____

How a Bill Becomes a Law © 2008 by Pat Luce and Holly Joyner, Scholastic Teaching Resources

100th Mock Congress
1st Session

H.R. _____
(number)

To_____

_____

(purpose of the bill)

In the House of Representatives

_____

(date)

Presented by the _____

(committee name)

A Bill

Be it enacted by the Senate and House of Representatives of the United States of America in Congress assembled,

_____

_____

_____

_____

_____

_____

_____

How a Bill Becomes a Law © 2008 by Pat Luce and Holly Joyner, Scholastic Teaching Resources

(continued on next page)

(continued)

100th Mock Congress
1st Session

_____

_____

_____

_____

_____

_____

_____

_____

_____

The Congressional Representative from

_____

The Congressional Representative from

_____

The Congressional Representative from

_____

The Congressional Representative from

_____

How a Bill Becomes a Law © 2008 by Pat Luce and Holly Joyner, Scholastic Teaching Resources

Dear Senator:

As the representative to our class from the state of _____,
you can teach us a little bit about your home state. Please complete the following
information.

State: _____

Capital: _____

Other major cities: _____

State nickname: _____

Where is it located in the United States?

_____

_____

Are there any major landforms or landmarks? (e.g., the Grand Canyon, Sears Tower)

_____

_____

_____

What are the names of the two U.S. Senators from your state?

_____

_____

OPTIONAL

How many delegates does your state send to the House of Representatives? _____

How a Bill Becomes a Law © 2008 by Pat Luce and Holly Joyner, Scholastic Teaching Resources

Name: _____   Date: _____

Dear Representative:

As the representative to our class from the state of _____,
you can teach us a little bit about your home state. Please complete the following
information.

State: _____

Capital: _____

Other major cities: _____

State nickname: _____

Where is it located in the United States?

_____

_____

Are there any major landforms or landmarks? (e.g., the Grand Canyon, Sears Tower)

_____

_____

_____

What is the name of one of the U.S. Representatives from your state?

_____

OPTIONAL

How many delegates does your state send to the House of Representatives? _____

How a Bill Becomes a Law © 2008 by Pat Luce and Holly Joyner, Scholastic Teaching Resources

This Assembly Will Now Come to Order!

OVERVIEW

Students present their bills to their respective chambers and debate the details of each bill. They will then vote on the bills to see which ones can move on to the other chamber and which ones need to go back to its committee for revision.

BEFORE YOU START

If possible, type up the bills that students wrote in the last episode and assign each one a number, such as H.R. 1 (House Bill 1) or S. 3 (Senate Bill 3). Have students from each bill's committee sign their names on their completed bills. Make enough copies of the bills for all members of Congress (i.e., students in the class) and distribute. Also, photocopy the voting cards on page 46 and distribute to students.

Arrange the room to replicate the two chambers of Congress. Set half of the chairs and desks on one side of the room for the Representatives and the rest on the other side for the Senators. Have committee members sit together. Create name cards for each student, making sure to include the state he or she represents, and place the appropriate cards on the table or desk in front of students. You will take on the roles of both the Speaker of the House and the President of the Senate, and you will sit in front facing Congress. You should also have a name card as either the Speaker of the House or President of the Senate, depending on who you are portraying. If you have access to a gavel, bring one to announce the start of the session.

Before the formal session begins, distribute copies of the Parliamentary Procedures (page 44) and Rules of Conduct (page 45) and go over them with the class.

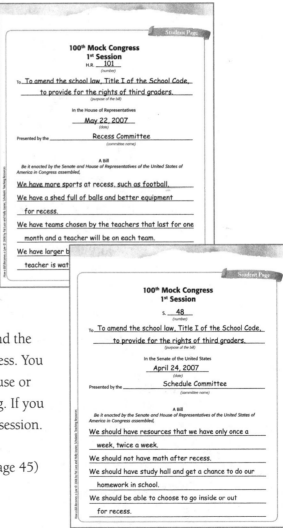

Parliamentary Procedures

1. Committee introduces and reads the bill.

2. Congress members can make a total of three comments (positive or negative) about the bill.

3. Committee responds to the comments.

4. A vote for the bill is called in the originating chamber.

5. If the bill passes in the originating chamber, it goes to the other chamber for another vote. If the bill does not pass, it goes back to the committee for revision.

6. Bills that pass both chambers go the President.

ALL VOTES ARE FINAL!

Rules of Conduct

1. Address the teacher as "Madam or Mister Speaker" (for the House of Representatives) or "Madam or Mister President" (for the Senate).

2. Address one another using the state that each Congressperson represents. For example, "My worthy fellow Senator from Wyoming" or "I yield to the Representative from Kentucky."

3. Once the debate has started, the House Speaker/Senate President will recognize the first member to speak by calling his or her state (e.g., "The chair recognizes the Senator from Vermont").

4. A member may not speak unless recognized by the House Speaker/Senate President. If another member is speaking at the time, the House Speaker/Senate President must first ask if that member will yield the floor to the new member. The speaking member does not have to yield the floor if the new member only wants to ask a question.

5. A member may speak only twice on any one bill being debated.

6. The House Speaker/Senate President may set a time limit on any debate or for any individual member.

7. After the debate is finished, either by time limit or a call for a vote by the House Speaker/Senate President, the vote is taken. The vote can be done by a show of hands with votes for passing a bill saying "Yea" and votes against the bill saying "Nay." The vote can also be taken by having each Congressperson fill in a voting card and the House Speaker/Senate President tallying the votes.

8. The House Speaker/Senate President announces the outcome of the vote.

RUNNING THE SIMULATION

To begin the session, the Speaker of the House or the President of the Senate (you, the teacher) will call for a report from the various committees. Strike the gavel (if you have one) and announce, "This assembly will now come to order as a committee of the whole for the purpose of considering the bills before it. The *[committee name]* will now read its report." Invite the members of the committee to stand and introduce themselves along with the names of the states they represent. Then the chairperson of the committee, as chosen by its members, reads their bill. Other members of the chamber should have a copy of the bill so they can read along. Instruct members of the other chamber to pay attention because they may have to present the bill to their chamber when it comes there for voting in the next episode.

After the bill has been read, debate begins with the House Speaker/Senate President recognizing the first member who raises his or her hand to speak. Committee members may respond to three questions or comments from their chamber and any comments or questions the House Speaker/Senate President might have.

When the discussion or debate is finished, the House Speaker/Senate President calls for a vote to decide the fate of the bill. If the bill originated in the House, the Representatives vote first. If it originated in the Senate, Senators get to vote first. Have students check "yea" or "nay" on their voting cards to signify their vote. After collecting the voting cards, count them and inform Congress of the results. There are two possible voting outcomes:

Response to H.R. 105　　　**VETOED**

To:　Supplies for Learning Committee – Representatives Epstein-Martin, Maddrey and West

Date:　May 25, 2007

I am in agreement with some of the provisions of this bill:

1. Bathrooms should be clean.

2. Keeping copies of Book Club books is possible only if inexpensive books can be found within teachers' budgets.

3. Every student could have a water bottle. Contacting the Parent Association regarding the costs, and finding monies to purchase the bottles would be a student initiative.

4. Some common areas have chalkboards and/or white boards. Each common area should have one.

5. Math games are a lot of fun and a great way to learn. Teachers and students should spend some time looking at the available games and adding, as needed.

I do not support the following provisions for these reasons:

1. Additional water fountains on the floors, color copiers, lockers and laptops are financially prohibitive, as well as impractical. The wait to use water fountains would decrease if students had water bottles. To tear out the cubbies in the school and purchase lockers is not the best use of funds. We can't afford a color copier for the faculty room. Consider the time spent on computers during school, and think about how laptops would be used. Think of the age of students. My question is what would be the best use of our technology monies.

2. The school's policy on the use of the Internet is developed according to developmental and educational guidelines. Student sites are approved by the Primary Division Director. Students have access to these sites. Teachers can submit sites they would like for approval.

I would like to thank the House Supplies for Learning Committee, the Honorables Epstein-Martin, Maddrey, and West for their thoughtful work and well-written suggestions.

Response to S.R. 105　　　**PASSED**

To:　Courtyard and Animals Committee – Senators Culp, Farquhar and Sisson

Date:　May 25, 2007

I am in agreement with both provisions of this bill:

1. The pond water should be checked on a regular basis for cleanliness.

2. More fish should be added to the pond when older fish die. The number of fish should be regulated to assure that there is enough food for all living creatures.

I would like to thank the Courtyard and Animals Committee, the Honorables Culp, Farquhar and Sisson, for their thoughtful work and well-written suggestions in revising the bill.

- The bill passes in the originating chamber by a majority vote (one more than half of the members). The bill will then go to the other chamber for a vote in the next episode.

- The bill does not pass in the originating chamber. It goes back to the committee for revision.

Following is an example of how a session might be conducted after a committee has read its bill to the members of Congress:

Teacher: All right, after hearing the report of the Ways and Means Committee on House Bill H.R. 101 the floor is now open to discussion and debate. *[Several students raise their hands, and the teacher points to one of them.]* The chair recognizes the Representative from Utah.

Representative from Utah: Ms. Lewis, I mean, Madam Speaker, I don't like the way that the bill spends money for stuff that we don't need.

Teacher: Could you explain what you mean?

Representative from Utah: I mean, why should we spend money for different kinds of food for school lunch when lots of kids bring lunch from home? *[Other students begin waving their hands, wanting to talk.]*

Teacher: Does the Representative from Utah yield the floor?

Representative from Utah: Oh, yeah, I guess so.

Teacher: The chair recognizes the Representative from Kentucky.

Representative from Kentucky: I don't agree. Lots of us want better lunches, and we think that it's worth the extra money. *[Lots of cheers from the class]*

Teacher: *(banging gavel)* Come to order! Does the Representative from Kentucky have any further comments? *[Student shakes her head.]* Then the chair will hear further arguments or comments for five more minutes, and then we will take a vote on H.R. 101. Does anyone have any other comments? *[Two students raise their hands.]*

This example shows how you can run the session in order to make the proceedings feel realistic. Participating in a structured debate that is very similar to what actually happens in Congress helps students gain a better understanding of exactly how the process works.

Alternate hearing bills between the House and the Senate so that no one stays out of action for too long. After all the bills have been voted on, ask the committees whose bills did not pass to work on revising them. Have committee members work together to revise and rewrite their bills, taking into account the comments made by other members of Congress and the House Speaker/Senate President during the session. Instruct committee members to clarify confusing language, make additions, or remove sections with the goal of having their bill pass both chambers of Congress in the next session. Have committees use the form on pages 47–48 (for the Senate) or pages 49–50 (House) to keep track of questions or concerns raised as well as suggested amendments to the bill.

As House Speaker/Senate President, you might want to play an active role in helping students with their revisions by responding in writing to the rejected bills. Such responses can give students insight into the reasons for certain school policies, how the faculty and administration make their decisions, and how change occurs in the school environment.

Circulate through the room to assist groups with changes and help them create solid, revised bills. Have students type or neatly handwrite their revised bills, ready for presentation in the next episode.

Parliamentary Procedures

1. Committee introduces and reads the bill.

2. Congress members can make a total of three comments (positive or negative) about the bill.

3. Committee responds to the comments.

4. A vote for the bill is called in the originating chamber.

5. If the bill passes in the originating chamber, it goes to the other chamber for another vote. If the bill does not pass, it goes back to the committee for revision.

6. Bills that pass both chambers go the President.

ALL VOTES ARE FINAL!

How a Bill Becomes a Law © 2008 by Pat Luce and Holly Joyner, Scholastic Teaching Resources

Rules of Conduct

1. Address the teacher as "Madam or Mister Speaker" (for the House of Representatives) or "Madam or Mister President" (for the Senate).

2. Address one another using the state that each Congressperson represents. For example, "My worthy fellow Senator from Wyoming" or "I yield to the Representative from Kentucky."

3. Once the debate has started, the House Speaker/Senate President will recognize the first member to speak by calling his or her state (e.g., "The chair recognizes the Senator from Vermont").

4. A member may not speak unless recognized by the House Speaker/ Senate President. If another member is speaking at the time, the House Speaker/Senate President must first ask if that member will yield the floor to the new member. The speaking member does not have to yield the floor if the new member only wants to ask a question.

5. A member may speak only twice on any one bill being debated.

6. The House Speaker/Senate President may set a time limit on any debate or for any individual member.

7. After the debate is finished, either by time limit or a call for a vote by the House Speaker/Senate President, the vote is taken. The vote can be done by a show of hands with votes for passing a bill saying "Yea" and votes against the bill saying "Nay." The vote can also be taken by having each Congressperson fill in a voting card and the House Speaker/Senate President tallying the votes.

8. The House Speaker/Senate President announces the outcome of the vote.

How a Bill Becomes a Law © 2008 by Pat Luce and Holly Joyner, Scholastic Teaching Resources

Voting Cards

Voting Card

Bill title: _____

YEA	NAY

Voting Card

Bill title: _____

YEA	NAY

How a Bill Becomes a Law © 2008 by Pat Luce and Holly Joyner, Scholastic Teaching Resources

Name: _____   Date: _____

From Bill to Law Recording Sheet (Senate)

Names of Senators:

Senator _____   from _____

Senator _____   from _____

Senator _____   from _____

Senator _____   from _____

Bill Number: _____

Questions _____
_____
_____
_____

Concerns _____
_____
_____

Suggested Amendments _____
_____
_____

1st VOTE

YEA	NAY

Additional Amendments _____
_____
_____

How a Bill Becomes a Law © 2008 by Pat Luce and Holly Joyner, Scholastic Teaching Resources

From Bill to Law Recording Sheet *(continued)*

2nd VOTE

YEA	NAY

Questions _____

_____

_____

_____

Concerns _____

_____

_____

Suggested Amendments _____

_____

_____

3rd VOTE

YEA	NAY

How a Bill Becomes a Law © 2008 by Pat Luce and Holly Joyner, Scholastic Teaching Resources

From Bill to Law Recording Sheet (House of Representatives)

Names of Representatives:

Representative _____   from _____

Representative _____   from _____

Representative _____   from _____

Representative _____   from _____

Bill Number: _____

Questions _____

_____

_____

_____

Concerns _____

_____

_____

Suggested Amendments _____

_____

_____

1st VOTE

YEA	NAY

Additional Amendments _____

_____

_____

How a Bill Becomes a Law © 2008 by Pat Luce and Holly Joyner, Scholastic Teaching Resources

Student Page

From Bill to Law Recording Sheet *(continued)*

2nd VOTE

YEA	NAY

Questions _____
_____
_____
_____

Concerns _____
_____
_____

Suggested Amendments _____
_____
_____

3rd VOTE

YEA	NAY

How a Bill Becomes a Law © 2008 by Pat Luce and Holly Joyner, Scholastic Teaching Resources

Episode 4

Vote or Veto?

OVERVIEW

Students whose bills did not pass in the last episode present their revised bills in their respective chambers. After another vote is taken, bills that pass move on to the other chamber for voting. A bill that passes in both chambers then goes to the President of the United States to be either signed into law or vetoed.

BEFORE YOU START

If possible, type up the bills that students revised in the last episode. Have students from each bill's committee sign their names on their revised bills. Make enough copies for all members of Congress and distribute. Also, photocopy the voting cards on page 46 and distribute to students.

Arrange the room as you did for Episode 3, with the desks set up to represent the two chambers of Congress. Before the formal session begins, go over the Parliamentary Procedures and Rules of Conduct with the class (pages 44 and 45).

BACKGROUND: THE EXECUTIVE BRANCH

The Constitution of the United States established a government with three branches—legislative, judicial, and executive. Each branch of government has its own specific jobs, and no single branch is more powerful than the others; they balance each other out. For example, the President (executive branch) offsets the legislative branch by having the power to veto bills and balances the judicial branch by appointing all federal judges, including the Supreme Court. The executive branch is the only branch of government in which most of the power is held by one person, the President of the United States.

As chief executive of our government, the President has many different responsibilities. The Constitution states that the President "shall take care that the laws be faithfully executed." This means the President is responsible for all law enforcement agencies in the United States, including the Federal Bureau of Investigation (FBI), the National Security Council, the Department of Justice, and many others. In addition, the President uses departments, such as the Environmental Protection Agency, to ensure that laws are being obeyed. One of the most important jobs of the President is to serve as the Commander-in-Chief of our military. That means that the President is in charge of all our armed forces—the Army, Navy, Air Force, Marines, and other military services. The President is also the chief diplomat of the United States and makes treaties and agreements with other governments. He or she can appoint ambassadors to foreign countries and use departments such as the Federal Trade Commission to negotiate treaties and agreements with those nations.

To help the President with all the job's responsibilities, he or she appoints a Cabinet—a group of people who advises the President on different matters. For instance, if a problem arises with another country, the President would ask the Secretary of State for advice. If the President needs advice about schools and education, he or she would ask the Secretary of Education. One of the most important members of the President's Cabinet is the Vice President. If for any reason the President cannot do his or her job, the Vice President takes over and becomes the President of our country. This has happened nine times so far in our history, most recently in 1974 when then-Vice President Gerald Ford took over the office after President Richard Nixon resigned.

So what does it take to become President and live in the White House? To qualify for this important job, a person must be a natural-born citizen of the United States, be at least 35 years of age, and have resided in the United States for at least 14 years. Once elected, the President serves a term of four years and may be reelected only once.

RUNNING THE SIMULATION

The Speaker of the House or the President of the Senate (you, the teacher) starts the session by reviewing the status of the bills before Congress—which bills went back to committees for revision and which bills will be presented to the other chamber of Congress by their committees for the first time.

Strike the gavel (if you have one) and announce, "This assembly will now come to order as a committee of the whole for the purpose of considering the bills before it. The *[committee name]* will now read its report." Start with the bills that have been revised. These bills should be presented in its originating chamber. Invite the members of the committee to stand and introduce themselves along with the names of the states they represent. Then the chairperson of the committee reads their revised bill. Other members of the chamber should have a copy of the bill so they can read along.

After the bill has been read, debate begins as in Episode 3, with the House Speaker/Senate President recognizing the first member who raises his or her hand to speak. Committee members may respond to three questions or comments from Congress and any comments or questions the House Speaker/Senate President might have. Debate on revised bills should be fairly brief, going over points that were revised.

When the discussion or debate is finished, the House Speaker/Senate President calls for a vote to decide the fate of the bill. Have students check "yea" or "nay" on their voting cards to signify their vote. After collecting the voting cards, count them and inform the Congress of the results.

- If the revised bill passes in the originating chamber by a majority vote (one more than half of the members), it will move on to the other chamber for a vote.

- If the revised bill does not pass in the originating chamber, it automatically dies.

At this point, all bills that have passed in its originating chamber will go to the other chamber for a vote. The bills should go to the counterpart committees in the other chamber. For example, a bill from the Senate's Finance Committee should go to the Committee on Appropriations in the House of Representatives. You may have to temporarily reassign the committees in each chamber so that they correspond to the original committees from the other chamber.

Have the various committees present the bills they received to their respective chambers. Alternate hearing bills between the House and the Senate so that no one has to stay out of the action for too long. After each bill has been presented, call for a vote to see if the bill passes this second chamber. Have students check "yea" or "nay" on their voting cards to signify their vote. After collecting the voting cards, count them and inform the Congress of the results.

- If the bill passes in the second chamber, it will go to the President of the United States (role-played by you or another teacher or, if possible, the school principal) for his or her consideration. The President may sign the bill into law at this point or veto it with suggestions for revisions.

- If the bill does not pass in the second chamber, it goes back to the committee (in the second chamber) for revision.

As President of the United States, be prepared to pass some bills and veto others. Choose a couple of bills to veto with suggestions on how to improve the bill. Students will go through the veto override process in the next episode.

Who Has the Final Say?

OVERVIEW

Students find out whether or not their bill gets signed into law. They also get to witness the system of checks and balances at work—as the President exercises his or her power to veto a bill, as Congress votes to override this veto, and as the Supreme Court Justices decide on the constitutionality of a law.

BACKGROUND: THE JUDICIAL BRANCH

The judicial branch of the United States government consists of the Supreme Court and the lower federal courts. The judicial branch, and specifically the Supreme Court, is the "watchdog" of our government. As the highest and most influential court, the Supreme Court is the guardian and interpreter of the United States Constitution, making sure that it is not abused or misused by the other two branches of government.

The Supreme Court and other courts of the judicial branch hear cases that challenge or require interpretation of the bills passed by Congress and signed into law by the President. The Court can also invalidate legislation from Congress and even overturn executive decisions made by the President when the Court feels that they are in conflict with the Constitution. The Supreme Court's decisions are final and can be overturned only by a constitutional amendment or a later decision by the Supreme Court.

The executive and legislative branches have powers that balance the power of the Supreme Court. The President nominates its Justices as well as other court judges, and the Senate ratifies (approves) or rejects those nominees. If approved by the Senate, the appointees to the federal bench serve for life or until they retire or resign. The average term for a Justice in the Supreme Court is 15 years. The longest-serving Justice was William O. Douglas, who retired in 1975 after serving for 36 years and 7 months. As of 2007, only 108 Justices have served in the Supreme Court, even though it has been in existence for more than 200 years.

Very little has changed since the Supreme Court was first established in 1790. Back then the Court consisted of five Associate Justices and a Chief Justice. Today there are eight Associate Justices and one Chief Justice. The Justices still wear black robes and quill pens are still placed on the counsel tables. And before every session of the court the Justices all shake hands in a tradition called "The Conference Handshake," which symbolizes that even though they may not all agree on cases before the court, they are united in their purpose to ensure the common good.

The Supreme Court begins its session on the first Monday in October and hears cases until June or July. More than 7,000 civil and criminal cases are filed with the Court each year. The lawyers for each side of a case have 30 minutes to make their arguments. There is no jury, and no witnesses are summoned. The Court, however, has extensive background information on all previous decisions that have been made concerning the case being argued.

The Court is dedicated to maintaining a balance between society's need for order and the individual's right to freedom. Engraved above the entrance to the Supreme Court building in Washington, D.C., are the words "Equal Justice Under Law." These words show the deep commitment that the Court has to the Rule of Law, democracy, and a constitutional republic.

BEFORE YOU START

In the last episode some bills went to the President (you or another teacher or the principal) for signing or vetoing. Choose two bills to veto and have them ready for debate at a joint session of Congress. Be sure to state reasons why the bills are being vetoed. Photocopy the bills and distribute to students.

Once again, arrange the room to replicate the two chambers of Congress. Set half of the chairs and desks on one side of the room for the Representatives and the rest on the other side for the Senators. Place appropriate name cards (with respective state names) on the table or desk in front of students. The President will sit in front facing Congress with a name card that identifies the person as the President of the United States. When the debating starts, the Speaker of the House or the President of the Senate (you) will take the place vacated by the President and sit in front of Congress.

Before the formal session begins, go over the Parliamentary Procedures and Rules of Conduct with the class (pages 44 and 45).

RUNNING THE SIMULATION

Tell students that the President will be presenting the new laws that he or she has signed, using the Public Law form on page 61. The President will also be presenting bills that he or she has decided to veto.

Inform students that this is a joint session of Congress—both the House and Senate are meeting together—for the purpose of deciding whether or not to override a presidential veto. Strike the gavel (if you have one) and announce, "This assembly will now come to order as a committee of the whole for the purpose of considering the vetoed bill before it. I will now read the veto." After the vetoed bill has been read, debate begins with the House Speaker/Senate President (you, the teacher) recognizing the first member who raises his or her hand to speak. Debate lasts until a vote is called for and the fate of the bill is decided.

Following is an example of how a session might be conducted after the President has vetoed a bill:

President of the United States: Good morning. I have before me H.R. 101. It was passed by both Houses of Congress and went to me for a signature. However, I have vetoed the bill for the following reasons:

1. H.R. 101 does not say how the new school lunch program will be funded.

2. H.R. 101 does not set any guidelines as to what new food would be offered to replace the current menu or who would select the new menu.

3. H.R. 101 only addresses the needs of those students who buy school lunch and excludes the concerns of those students who bring lunch from home.

House Speaker/Senate President: The floor is now open for debate before a final veto override vote. Remember that 2/3 of all of the Senate and House of Representatives must vote for the bill in order to override the President's veto. *[Students raise their hands to speak.]* The chair recognizes the Senator from Texas.

Senator from Texas: Madam Speaker, I think that the President is wrong. If students don't like the school lunch, they just throw it away and that's a waste.

Representative from Utah: That's not what the problem—

House Speaker/Senate President: The Senator from Texas has the floor. You can't just interrupt. Does the Senator from Texas yield the floor?

Senator from Texas: Yes.

House Speaker/Senate President: The chair recognizes the Representative from Utah.

Representative from Utah: Sorry for butting in, but I don't agree. He *[pointing at the Senator from Texas]* didn't answer the problems that the President had with the bill. I don't think that it would be a fair law either.

House Speaker/Senate President: Will the Representative from Utah yield the floor for further comments? *[Student nods.]* Then the chair will hear further arguments or comments for five more minutes, and then we will take a vote on overriding the President's veto of H.R. 101. Does anyone have any other comments? *[Several students raise their hands.]*

After the discussion is finished, call for a vote to decide the fate of the bill. Have students check "yea" or "nay" on their voting cards to signify their vote. Remind students that in order to override a veto, 2/3 of Congress must vote for the bill to pass. After collecting the voting cards, count them and inform Congress of the results.

- If the bill passes in Congress, fill out the Law Form without the President's signature.

- If the bill fails, it dies.

Move on to the second vetoed bill and repeat the process of debate and voting. Remember to veto only two bills at the most so that students get a feel for the process but the session does not drag on for too long.

TAKING IT FURTHER: HERE COME THE JUDGES . . .

When the second debate is over and the vote has been taken, inform the class that the Supreme Court has decided to question the constitutionality of one of the new laws. (Or if you prefer, use the sample case provided on pages 59–60 to discuss.) Choose the law that you think is the most marginal for constitutionality and explain what that term means. For instance, does one of the laws possibly infringe on someone's rights? Does it put one person or group's interests over someone else's interests, even if the intent was well meaning?

Read aloud the details of the case to the class, leaving out the arguments for the prosecution and defense. Choose nine students to serve as the Supreme Court Justices, then assign two groups of four or five students each to act as opposing counsels who would debate whether or not the law is constitutional. You might have students use the Bill of Rights to base their debate upon. Give students some time to build their arguments. While students are discussing within their groups, rearrange the class to represent the Supreme Court chambers with seats for the nine Justices at the front behind desks or tables and two tables across from them for the opposing counsels. Set up a row of chairs behind them for a gallery of students not directly involved in the debate. You could also have these students represent the press corps, taking notes about the proceedings for publication in their papers.

Before the court session begins, have the Justices wait outside the classroom and shake hands before entering the room. Have the rest of the class stand up as you bang the gavel and announce, "The Honorable, the Chief Justice and the Associate Justices of the Supreme Court of the United States. Oyez! Oyez! Oyez! All persons having business before the Honorable, the Supreme Court of the United States, are admonished to draw near and give their attention, for the court is now sitting. God save the United States and this Honorable Court!"

Acting as court clerk, formally read the case to the court. Allow each side 5 minutes to make their arguments regarding the constitutionality of the law. (Inform students that in the actual Supreme Court, both sides have only 30 minutes each to make their arguments.) Allow the Justices to meet privately so they can render a decision by voting. Remind the Justices to make a decision based on what the two sides said and whether they feel the law is or is not constitutional. Majority vote wins, meaning that at least five of the Justices must agree on a decision. After their private vote the Chief Justice (the student sitting in the middle) reads the decision of the court.

Simulation Wrap-Up

Give each student a copy of the Congressional Record (page 62). Have students write about their experience over the course of the simulation. Instruct them to write in the first person as if they were really the Representative or Senator whom they have been portraying. Use this Congressional Record as an assessment tool to determine just how much students have learned about our government. You might also want to hand out photocopies of the worksheet on page 63 as part of your assessment to see if students truly understand how a bill becomes a law.

Answers (page 63): 5, 3, 10, 1, 7, 4, 11, 9, 6, 2, 8

Sample Case:
The Anti-Bullying Act

OVERVIEW

Last year, School Congress passed H.R. 103, "The Anti-Bullying Act," and the President signed it into law. Last week, fifth-grade student Rachel challenged the law as unconstitutional. Rachel v. The School has now reached the Supreme Court and will be heard by that court.

Amendment VI (from The Bill of Rights)

In all criminal prosecutions, the accused shall enjoy the right to a speedy and public trial, by an impartial jury of the State and district wherein the crime shall have been committed, which district shall have been previously ascertained by law, and to be informed of the nature and cause of the accusation; to be confronted with the witnesses against him; to have compulsory process for obtaining witnesses in his favor, and to have the Assistance of Counsel for his defence.

School Government Code ~ 12B "The Anti-Bullying Act"

"A person who has been reported as engaging in bullying by a student or students shall serve 1 (one) day of in-school detention and have their guardian notified in the interest of public safety."

BACKGROUND

This law was enacted because of a rise in the number of bullying incidents in school. Many students and parents had voiced their concerns that children were not feeling safe and even avoided going to school because they were afraid of being bullied. A bill was written with the intent of stopping this growing problem. The School Congress passed the bill and the President signed it into law to go into effect at the beginning of this school year.

How a Bill Becomes a Law © 2008 by Pat Luce and Holly Joyner, Scholastic Teaching Resources

SAMPLE CASE: THE ANTI-BULLYING ACT *(continued)*

THE CASE

The law was recently challenged when Rachel was given detention for bullying, and her mother was called by the principal. In addition to detention, Rachel was grounded for a week by her mother. Rachel has accused the school government of passing a law that violates her rights under the 6th Amendment to the Constitution because she was never allowed "to be confronted with the witnesses against her." She contends that a student or students with a personal vendetta are falsely accusing her in order to "get her into trouble."

The school argues that Rachel's bullying has caused students to keep silent for fear that if they speak up, they'll be known as tattletales; but more important, they fear retribution from both Rachel and her friends.

The Federal Court records show that no actual physical harm has been done to any students by Rachel, and Rachel has no prior offenses in past grades for bullying.

Each side has 15 minutes to prepare their arguments for the court and 5 minutes to make those arguments to the bench. The Justices must then withdraw and have 10 minutes to write their decision as to the Constitutionality of the law.

Points for the Defense to Argue

- The 6th Amendment guarantees the right to face your accuser.
- The 6th Amendment also guarantees the right to bring witnesses to speak in your defense, and Rachel was not given this right.
- No one was harmed.
- There is nothing in the law to protect the rights of the accused.

Points for the Prosecution to Argue

- Bullying is a very serious problem in schools.
- Victims of bullying will not come forward if they think that it will lead to more bullying.
- *Preventing* bullying is a much better idea than *allowing* bullying to occur.
- The law is not overly punitive and is a wake-up call that says, "We take bullying seriously at this school."

How a Bill Becomes a Law © 2008 by Pat Luce and Holly Joyner, Scholastic Teaching Resources

Public Law

Public Law _____
(number)

100th Mock Congress

An Act

To _____

_____

_____
(purpose of the law)

   Be it enacted by the Senate and House of Representatives of the United States of America in Congress assembled,

_____

_____

_____

_____

_____

_____

_____

_____

_____

Approved

_____
(date)

How a Bill Becomes a Law © 2008 by Pat Luce and Holly Joyner, Scholastic Teaching Resources

Congressional Record

_____

_____

_____

_____

_____

_____

_____

_____

_____

_____

_____

_____

_____

_____

_____

_____

_____

Faithfully Submitted by _____
(name)

On This Day _____
(date)

How a Bill Becomes a Law © 2008 by Pat Luce and Holly Joyner, Scholastic Teaching Resources

How a Bill Becomes a Law

Directions: Listed below are the steps necessary for a bill to become a law, but they are all mixed up. Number the steps so that they are in the correct order.

	The bill goes to the House, where it is debated.
	The bill is sent to the appropriate committee for consideration.
	The President signs the bill.
	An interest group proposes an idea for a law.
	The House votes on the bill.
	The committee holds a hearing on the bill and votes on it.
	The bill becomes a law!
	The Senate votes on the bill.
	The House committee changes or amends bill, if necessary.
	A Representative introduces the bill to the House.
	The bill is sent to the Senate.

How a Bill Becomes a Law © 2008 by Pat Luce and Holly Joyner, Scholastic Teaching Resources

References

Books

Making Laws: A Look at How a Bill Becomes a Law
by Sandy Donovan
(Lerner Publishing Group, 2003)

How Congress Works: A Look at the Legislative Branch
by Ruth Tenzer Feldman
(Lerner Publishing Group, 2003)

Congress (Watts Library)
by Suzanne Levert
(Franklin Watts, 2005)

The Kid's Guide to Social Action
by Barbara A. Lewis
(Free Spirit Publishing, 1998)

A More Perfect Union: The Story of Our Constitution
by Betsy Maestro and Giulio Maestro
(Collins, 2008)

Constitution Translated for Kids
by Cathy Travis
(Synergy Books, 2006)

Video

Schoolhouse Rock! America Rock
Directed by Tom Warburton
(Walt Disney Video, 1973)

Web Sites

Ben's Guide to U.S. Government (6–8): How Laws Are Made
http://bensguide.gpo.gov/6-8/lawmaking/index.html

Kids in the House – How Laws Are Made
http://clerkkids.house.gov/laws/index.html

Project Vote Smart – GOVERNMENT 101: How a Bill Becomes a Law
http://www.vote-smart.org/resource_govt1011_pt02.php

THOMAS (Legislative Information from the Library of Congress)
http://thomas.loc.gov/

United States House of Representatives
http://www.house.gov/

U.S. Senate
http://www.senate.gov/